Echoes That Built Eternity

Poems on the Soul's Eternal Architecture

Daksh Siwasia

/ BookLeaf
Publishing

India | USA | UK

Made with ❤ on the BookLeaf Publishing Platform
www.bookleafpub.in
www.bookleafpub.com

Dedication

*For those who keep the flame alive
when the night grows longest.*

Preface

This book is more than a collection of poems. It is a journey — from the first light of childhood to the shadows that shape us, from the wounds that leave scars to the fire that carries us forward. Within these pages live the dreams that refused to die, the silences that spoke when words could not, and the stars that still burn when everything else has faded.

I did not write these poems as monuments, but as companions — for the quiet nights, the heavy mornings, the moments when you need to be reminded that even in darkness, something within you still glows.

If you find yourself here — in the wound that became a window, in the mirror that remembers your soul, in the sky that still holds your wings — then these poems are no longer mine alone. They are ours.

To be human is to break and mend, to lose and rise, to walk through shadow and still carry light. That is the heartbeat of this book.

Acknowledgements

This book was never mine alone. It was shaped by every kindness that kept me moving, every silence that let me listen, and every shadow that showed me where the light begins.

To all who walked beside me — in life, in memory, or only for a fleeting moment — I owe more than words. Your presence became the fire that warmed me, the window that opened when hope was dim, the star that would not let me give up.

To you, the reader: these poems are unfinished until you breathe them in. If one line carries your own dream, your own silence, your own unbroken light, then this book has found its true home.

And above all, to the human soul we all share — fragile yet enduring, breakable yet luminous — my deepest gratitude. These words were never mine alone. They were always ours.

The Magic of Innocence

Once, the world was made of light,
A canvas bright with every sight—
The sky was painted just for play,
And stars, our friends, would always stay.

The grass beneath, so soft and green,
Held secrets whispered, yet unseen.
A touch, a laugh, a fleeting dream,
A life was lived in quiet gleam.

Hands that held the world so wide,
In pockets deep, no need to hide.
With eyes that sparkled, wide and true,
The world was ours—both me and you.

No rules were written, none to break,
Just endless fields for us to take,
Where we could run with endless grace,
And every step was full of space.

We spoke in words that held no weight,
Yet carried truths that would not wait—
A simple joy, a simple rhyme,
That echoed soft throughout all time.

But as I grew, the world grew cold,
The magic dimmed, the dreams grew old.
Yet in the quiet of the night,
I feel the spark, the child's delight.

For deep inside, that magic stays,
A glow that never quite decays.
And though I've grown, I'll always know—
That magic once, was ours to sow.

The Moment You Become You

Before the world told you who to be,
Before the names, the rules, the lies—
There was a moment, soft as air,
When you first saw through your own eyes.

A whisper louder than the rest,
A spark inside, a fire unspun,
And you, in all your fragile glory,
Became the *only* one.

Not who they said you had to be,
Not what they tried to make you do—
But *you*, raw and undefined,
A force that only *you* could choose.

The Dream That Refused to Die

It came to me when I was small,
A spark too fragile to recall.
It whispered softly in the night,
A secret flame, a borrowed light.

The years were heavy, winds grew wild,
The world demanded I grow mild.
They told me dreams were made for sleep,
For foolish hearts, for those too weak.

Yet still it stirred beneath my skin,
A gentle knocking from within.
Through broken days, through endless tries,
It lived where even hope had died.

And when my hands were torn with scars,
It traced new maps among the stars.
It held me up when I was low,
A voice that whispered, *"Still, you'll grow."*

Now I have seen the world's disguise,
The cost of truths, the weight of lies—
But one small ember still burns high:
The dream that never learned to die.

The Silence That Holds the Soul

There are moments when the world grows still,
When words collapse, too heavy to fill.
No voices rise, no echoes roll—
Just silence, cradling the soul.

It holds the grief we cannot say,
The love that time can't take away.
It gathers tears the eyes don't show,
A quiet river, soft and slow.

In silence lives the child I was,
The dreams that slept, the endless "because."
It keeps the questions never told,
The fragile truths I dared to hold.

It speaks in shadows, speaks in light,
A hidden prayer, a star at night.
It wraps me close, yet makes me whole—
The silence that sustains the soul.

And when the world demands my name,
When noise and burdens feel the same,
I close my eyes, let silence stay—
It holds me firm, and lights my way.

For silence is no empty place,
It is the heart's most sacred space.
A language deep, beyond control—
The silence that restores the soul.

The Wound That Became a Window

There was a crack I could not hide,
A fracture running deep inside.
It bled in silence, sharp and raw,
A wound the world could never saw.

At first, it felt like endless night,
A broken thing, devoid of light.
But through the pain, a whisper came,
Soft as ash, yet strong as flame.

The wound that tore my heart apart
Became a window to the heart.
Through shattered glass, the sky poured in,
And love broke open where grief had been.

I saw the stars not far, but near,
I heard the truth the soul holds dear:
That every scar, though born of strife,
Can carve a doorway into life.

So let me not conceal the scar,
For what I am is what we are.
A fragile frame, a tender whole,
The wound that made a window—
Saved my soul.

The Fire That Wouldn't Fade

It started small, a flicker's breath,
A glow that danced with life and death.
Through nights of cold, through storms of rain,
It burned through silence, burned through pain.

They tried to dim it, tried to say,
"No light can last, all flames decay."
But every whisper, every doubt,
Only made its embers shout.

I carried it when skies went black,
When every step pulled me back.
I fed it tears, I fed it scars,
And still it reached for higher stars.

It lit my hands when strength was gone,
It sang to me when hope moved on.
It warmed the places fear had chilled,
It built the dreams I swore I'd build.

And even now, though years have passed,
Though shadows stretch and time runs fast,
That fire still hums beneath my skin—
A voice that says, *"You will not give in."*

So if the night feels vast, unmade,
Remember this: flames may fade—
But somewhere deep, through ash and shade,
Burns the fire that won't be swayed.

The Shadow That Taught Me Light

I once cursed the dark that followed me,
its weight a chain I could not flee.
It whispered fears I tried to hide,
a colder self I kept inside.

But shadows are not just the night—
they bend, they shape, they frame the light.
And in their silence, soft and deep,
they guard the truths we fail to keep.

It was the shadow who taught me pain,
but also how to rise again.
It carved my scars into a song,
and showed me where I still belong.

For light alone can blind the eyes,
but shadow teaches where it lies—
in every crack, in every seam,
the darker half completes the dream.

So now I walk with both as one,
the dark, the dawn, the night, the sun.
For even grief can burn so bright—
the shadow taught me how to light.

The Sky That Remembered My Wings

There was a time I learned to crawl,
while dreams grew quiet, small, and tall.
The weight of earth pressed down so near,
and skies I loved forgot to hear.

My wings, once bright, were tucked away,
their feathers dimmed by night and day.
I walked with feet too heavy, slow,
forgetting winds that used to know.

But skies are patient, skies are kind,
they hold the things we leave behind.
And when I lifted weary eyes,
the clouds still waited, soft and wise.

A whisper rose from blue so deep:
"Your wings are not for dust to keep.
The storms you feared, they only bend,
they break, but also teach to mend."

And in that moment, air grew wide,
the sky stretched out its endless side.
It called me back to what was mine,
to rise, to fall, to trust, to climb.

So now I fly — not just for flight,
but for the dark that taught me light.
For even grounded souls can sing,
in skies that still remember wings.

The Mirror That Remembered My Soul

I stood before the glass one day,
expecting only lines of clay—
the weary face, the fleeting years,
the weight of time, the veil of tears.

But as I gazed, the surface stirred,
and whispered back without a word.
Not bone, not skin, not eyes grown old,
but something deeper, bright and bold.

It showed the child I used to be,
with eyes unchained, alive, and free—
who laughed at winds, who dreamed with skies,
who found the world in fireflies.

It showed the scars I tried to hide,
yet gave them wings and made them pride.
It turned my wounds to rivers wide,
where broken pieces learned to glide.

The mirror held what I forgot,
the flame that time had not yet caught.
Through cracks of loss, through years of role,
it still remembered all my soul.

And in its truth, I came to see,
the one I lost was always me.
No glass could fade, no years control,
The mirror still remembered whole.

The Roar That Shook the Silence

The plains lay still, the grasses bowed,
No whisper stirred, no heartbeat loud.
The sky held breath, the earth lay bare,
A waiting hush hung in the air.

Then from the depths of golden mane,
Thunder rolled, a sovereign flame.
A single sound, both fierce and wide,
It split the silence open.

The trees bent low, the rivers stirred,
The mountains answered what they heard.
Not rage alone, but life's command,
The voice of dust, of sky, of land.

Within that roar was hunger's cry,
The sting of loss, the strength to try,
A vow carried across night and sun,
That every dawn, the fight goes on.

Yet in his gaze, a gentler fire,
A quiet strength, a calm desire.
For even kings, though crowned with might,
Are bound by love to guard the light.

So when the silence comes again,
And grasses wait in breathless plain,
The echo lingers, deep, profound—
A soul remembered by its sound.

The Bridge That Held Two Worlds

It rose where rivers clawed the land,
a span of stone, of steel, of hand—
a silver arc against the sky,
where earth and dream were bound to meet.

Beneath it raged the waters deep,
that swallowed kings, that would not sleep.
Yet still it stood, through storm and flame,
a voice unbroken, bold in frame.

Caravans thundered, banners streamed,
merchants bartered, soldiers dreamed.
Children's laughter crossed its floor,
as strangers stepped through stranger's door.

It held the tread of pilgrim feet,
the clash of armies when they meet,
the songs of sailors home from war,

the cries of nations torn before.

By lantern light, by morning's gleam,
it bore the weight of every dream.
A thousand tongues, a thousand hands,
met halfway, where the stone still stands.

And though the empires rise and fall,
though ivy climbs the crumbled wall,
the bridge remains, a steadfast thread,
where two worlds touched, and hope was fed.

The Volcano That Buried a City

The morning broke with laughter's call,
children's footsteps raced through hall,
vendors sang of bread and wine,
the market thrummed with life divine.

But far above, the mountain stirred,
a muffled breath, a warning slurred.
The earth beneath began to moan,
a giant waking, flesh of stone.

Ash like whispers laced the sky,
darkening sun with sudden sigh.
Fires bloomed where shadows crept,
and towers wept where silence slept.

The fountains froze, the temples shook,
as molten rivers carved a new book.
Streets once bright with painted art
were torn apart, yet burned with heart.

Mothers held their children near,
fathers fought through smoke and fear.
A lover's hand, a friend's last call,
frozen mid-cry, became the wall.

The mountain roared, the heavens dimmed,
the sea withdrew, its edges rimmed.
In one great breath, the city fell,
entombed beneath the mountain's spell.

Yet still, beneath that hardened dome,
remain the echoes, flesh, and home.
Not death alone, but life remains,
preserved in ash, through fire's chains.

The city sleeps, yet speaks through dust,
its stories rise, its stones still trust.
A testament both fierce and fair—
the world remembers they were there.

The Wall That Heard the Wars

It stood in silence, stone on stone,
a sentinel shaped, yet all alone.
Through shifting years, through dust and flame,
it bore the weight, it kept the name.

It heard the clash of steel on steel,
the cries that begged, the boots that beat the earth.
It felt the tremor, smelled the fire,
as kingdoms rose, then did expire.

It caught the whispers in the night,
the secret plans, the vows to fight.
It held the echo, sharp and raw,
the shouts of men who carved the law.

It knew the banners bright and proud,
the drums that thundered far and loud.
It marked the silence when they fell,
and learned the cost no tongue could tell.

The wall still stands, though scarred and worn,
its edges cracked, its surface torn.
Yet every stone, though chipped with scars,
still holds the sound of human wars.

And should you lean with careful ear,
a thousand voices stir, and draw near.
Not ghosts, not myths, but truths that stay—
the wall remembers what we say.

The Mountain That Held the Gods

It rose where silence met the sky,
its crown of ice forever high.
No mortal foot could claim its crest,
yet legends swore the gods found rest.

Its walls were carved from flame and storm,
a throne where countless myths were born.
The winds would bow, the stars would stay,
to guard the peak till break of day.

Pilgrims came with songs of flame,
hearts alight with hushed desire.
They circled, but dared not climb,
the gate of gods, outside of time.

The rivers flowing from its side
were whispered prayers the earth supplied.
Each stream a voice, each stone a word,
a hymn the ageless heavens heard.

And when the thunder split the dome above,
the mountain stood, the gods' true home.
Unbroken, vast, it kept their will,
a sacred heart the world holds still.

The Tree That Bound Earth and Sky

Its roots sank deep in ancient stone,
where rivers hummed and seeds were sown.
The earth it held in quiet might,
a cradle drawn from shadowed night.

Its trunk, a tower carved by flame,
bore scars that time could not reclaim.
Through storm and drought, through age untold,
it stood, a guardian stern and bold.

Its branches rose where eagles fly,
their fingers brushed the painted sky.
Among the clouds, the stars would rest,
as dawn lay sleeping in its crest.

Beneath its shade, the nations met,
with songs that none could now forget.
The warrior laid aside his blade,
the mother knelt, the child still played.

When thunder rolled and heavens wept,
the faithful came, the silence kept.
They touched its bark, they kissed its frame,
and swore their lives within its name.

No crown of gold, no mortal throne,
could rival what this tree had grown.
For earth and sky in union lie,
bound by its breath, they shall not die.

And still it stands, though years decay,
a bridge where worlds find one true way.
Its roots below, its arms on high,
the tree that bound the earth and sky.

The Song That Built a Nation

It started soft, a simple thread,
a lullaby the mothers spread.
A note that rose from village flame,
and carried forth a people's name.

It marched with feet on dust-worn roads,
it lit the dark of tyrant's loads.
Through shackled night, through shadow's reign,
the song endured, a bright refrain.

The farmer hummed it in his field,
the soldier heard, his wound was healed.
The child at play, the elder's prayer,
all wove their voices through the air.

When cannons roared and sabers clashed,
the song rang out where banners flashed.
Not forged of steel, nor born of crown,
but in the hearts it could not drown.

It rose in halls of stone and fire,
it stirred the lowly to aspire.
Each verse a bridge, each chord a flame,
that bound the many into one name.

And when the dawn at last was free,
the anthem crowned their destiny.
A song once whispered, frail and small,
had built a nation, strong for all.

The Road That Led to Nowhere

It stretched beyond the edge of time,
through shattered stone, through dust and rhyme.
Its path was worn by countless feet,
by tears and songs the years repeat.

It bore the weight of war and peace,
of broken chains, of sudden release.
No throne, no crown, no victor's claim—
the road endured, yet stayed the same.

It heard the whispers lovers keep,
the vows they sow, the griefs they reap.
It carried dreams both lost and true,
and bore them on, as roads must do.

And though it led to nowhere's end,
it kept the lives it chose to send.
Each step remained, each story sown—
a path of all, yet claimed by none.

The Ship That Never Returned

It left the harbor, proud and tall,
its sails like wings, its flags a call.
The tide was kind, the skyline glowed,
it bore the hopes that never returned.

It crossed the nights, it crossed the years,
through laughter, song, through secret fears.
The ocean kept what hearts had yearned,
upon the ship that never returned.

The storms awoke, the dark winds cried,
the masts were torn, the compass lied.
The sea rose high, the heavens churned,
and claimed the ship that never returned.

The lanterns dimmed, the decks grew cold,
as whispers turned to prayers untold.
The sea drew tight, the heavens burned,
around the ship that never returned.

Yet still in towns along the shore,
they wait for steps that come no more.
For every tide, one truth is learned:
to mourn the ship that never returned.

The City That Sank Beneath the Waves

Its streets once rang with golden light,
with laughter clear, with torches bright.
But tides crept close, the earth betrayed,
and drowned the walls its people made.

The bells were stilled, the windows broke,
the sea rose high in thunder's cloak.
A thousand prayers the night still saves—
the city lost beneath the waves.

Yet when the moon on waters gleams,
the drowned still walk in broken dreams.
Their voices ride the ocean's graves—
the city sank beneath the waves.

The Tower That Swallowed the Storm

It rose from cliffs where tempests roared,
its stones unshaken, skyward soared.
Lightning struck, the thunder crashed,
yet in its heart, no stone was smashed.

The winds would wail, the torrents weep,
the tower held what storms could reap.
Its shadow sprawled across the plains,
a bastion wrought from fire and rains.

Sailors saw it from distant seas,
a lighthouse tall against the breeze.
They steered their ships through night and fear,
guided by walls that would not tear.

And when the clouds gave all they bore,
and heaven's wrath had spent its store,
the tower stood, a steadfast spine,
a hymn of might where storms entwine.

The Star That Refused to Die

It burned when empires turned to dust,
when swords were sheathed, when thrones would rust.
Through broken crowns and fleeting years,
its fire endured our hopes and fears.

The night grew black, the heavens dim,
yet still it sang its steadfast hymn.
No storm could shake, no shadow bind,
the light it gave to all mankind.

The sailor's chart, the pilgrim's flame,
the silent witness none could tame.
It watched the lost, it blessed the brave,
and lit the path through dark and grave.

And when the skies at last grow cold,
its final tale will still be told:
that in the void, one truth burns high—
the star that dared to not yet die.